ROBOTS EXPLORING SPACE

NEW HORIZONS

A Robot Explores Pluto and the Kuiper Belt

James Bow

PowerKiDS press™

NEW YORK

Published in 2017 by **The Rosen Publishing Group**
29 East 21ˢᵗ Street, New York, NY 10010

Produced for Rosen by Calcium

Editors for Calcium: Sarah Eason and Harriet McGregor
Designers for Calcium: Jennie Child
Picture researcher: Rachel Blount

Picture credits: Cover: NASA/JHU APL/SwRI/Steve Gribben (New Horizons image), Thinkstock:
Pixtum (top banner), Shutterstock: Andrey_Kuzmin (metal plate), Thinkstock: -strizh- (back
cover illustration); Inside: NASA: 11, 14, NASA, ESA, and G. Bacon (STScI) 29, Johns Hopkins
University Applied Physics Laboratory/Southwest Research Institute 12-13, 15, 18, 22-23, 25, 26;
Shutterstock: edobric 6-7, Christos Georghiou 9, Olga Popova 7 top; Wikimedia Commons: NASA,
ESA, and L. Frattare (STScI) 21, NASA/Kim Shiflett 17.

CATALOGING-IN-PUBLICATION DATA
Names: Bow, James.
Title: New horizons: a robot explores Pluto and the Kuiper Belt / James Bow.
Description: New York : Powerkids Press, 2017. | Series: Robots exploring space | Includes index.
Identifiers: ISBN 9781508151333 (pbk.) | ISBN 9781508151272 (library bound) |
    ISBN 9781508151166 (6 pack)
Subjects: LCSH: Kuiper Belt--Juvenile literature. | Solar system--Juvenile literature.
Classification: LCC QB695.B69 2017 | DDC 523.48--dc23

Manufactured in the United States of America
CPSIA Compliance Information: Batch #BS16PK. For Further Information contact Rosen Publishing, New York, New York at 1-800-237-9932

CONTENTS

The Mission

Robots are traveling to areas of space never before visited by humans. While people have traveled into space and even to the moon, space is a dangerous place for humans. They must bring air, water, and food with them. They need to build spacecraft that can hold all the equipment they need. And, in order to travel beyond Earth's **orbit** or the moon, spacecraft have to carry all the supplies people need for months, or even years at a time.

Robots are perfect for exploring space. They do not need food, water, or air. They can travel for years, perform tasks in space that humans cannot, and communicate, or send, their findings to people back on Earth.

Working Together

However, robots are not putting astronauts and scientists out of work! It takes dozens of scientists and engineers to design and build robots able to go into space. It takes even more scientists to guide the robots on their journeys and to look over the **data** the robots find.

Robot Journey

This book looks at the mission of a robot named *New Horizons*. This robot went on a journey to the farthest reaches of the solar system. The trip was so long that the planet it traveled to, Pluto, was no longer considered a planet by the time the robot got there! What it discovered answered many questions and raised new ones. It even changed the way we look at our solar system.

This is an artist's depiction of *New Horizons* nearing Pluto, with Charon in the background.

Groundwork

Pluto is 4.67 billion miles (7.5 billion km) from Earth so scientists knew it would be a challenge to explore. Mars, Venus, and Mercury are more than 100 times closer to Earth than Pluto, and much easier to visit. In the 1970s, however, the National Aeronautics and Space Administration (NASA) sent two probes named *Voyager 1* and *2* to the outer solar system, to take pictures of Jupiter and Saturn. Scientists thought about sending *Voyager 1* past Pluto, but they could not do that and still take a close look at Saturn's moon, Titan. *Voyager 2* visited Uranus and Neptune, but was too far away to carry out a Pluto **flyby**.

Looking at Pluto

By the time eight of the solar system's planets had been explored, scientists thought that Pluto should get some attention. There was also evidence that the planet's neighborhood was more interesting than first thought. There were signs of many icy, rocky objects, like a second **asteroid belt**. This area was named the **Kuiper belt**, after Gerard Kuiper (1905–1973), the astronomer who first suggested the asteroid belt might exist.

NASA wanted to explore Pluto, but found the mission would be expensive. However, as more objects were found in the Kuiper belt, pressure to fund a Pluto mission increased. In 2003, the U.S. government agreed to spend $700 million on a mission called *New Horizons*.

SPACE FIRST

PLUTO NOT YET EXPLORED **29**USA

A STAMP MAY HAVE INSPIRED THE MISSION TO PLUTO! IN OCTOBER 1991, THE U.S. POSTAL SERVICE RELEASED A SERIES OF STAMPS CELEBRATING NASA'S EXPLORATION OF THE SOLAR SYSTEM. EACH STAMP SHOWED A PLANET, AND THE NAME OF THE FIRST SPACECRAFT TO VISIT IT. PLUTO WAS SHOWN WITH THE WORDS "NOT YET EXPLORED" BENEATH IT. WORLD SPACE FEDERATION PRESIDENT ROBERT STAEHLE WAS AT THE STAMP UNVEILING, AND WAS INSPIRED TO DRAW UP PLANS FOR A MISSION TO PLUTO.

New Horizons was designed to fly to Pluto and the Kuiper belt, where the sun looks barely larger than other stars in the sky.

Planet or Not?

Until 1781, we only knew of six planets in our solar system: Mercury, Venus, Earth, Mars, Jupiter, and Saturn. These were the planets we could see with the naked human eye. Then, British astronomer William Herschel (1738–1822) looked through a telescope and saw Uranus. Scientists began looking for more new planets, using mathematical equations to predict where they could be found. In 1846, German astronomer Johann Gottfried Galle (1812–1910) used the equations of astronomers Urbain Le Verrier (1811–1877) and John Couch Adams (1819–1892) to find Neptune. The hunt for the ninth planet was then on!

An American Discovery

In the late 1920s, American Clyde Tombaugh (1906–1997) joined the hunt. He took photographs of the night sky, over many nights. Comparing these pictures of stars, he looked for any small dot that appeared to move across the photos. In 1930, he discovered Pluto, the smallest planet in the solar system and one that takes 246 years to orbit the sun.

SPACE DISCOVERY

CLYDE TOMBAUGH WAS AN AMERICAN FARM BOY WITH ONLY A HIGH SCHOOL EDUCATION WHEN HE DISCOVERED PLUTO IN 1930. HOWEVER, HE COULD BUILD HIS OWN TELESCOPES, AND GOT A JOB AT THE LOWELL OBSERVATORY, WHERE HE SPENT HOURS LOOKING FOR PLUTO. FOLLOWING HIS DISCOVERY, HE GOT HIS COLLEGE EDUCATION, TAUGHT ASTRONOMY, AND FOUND HUNDREDS OF ASTEROIDS.

Mercury
Venus
Earth
Mars
Jupiter
Saturn
Uranus
Neptune
Pluto

Image not to scale

From 1930 to 2006, diagrams showed our solar system with nine planets, and Pluto the farthest from the sun.

However, decades later, as planning for the *New Horizons* mission was taking place, some astronomers were wondering if Pluto should really be called a planet. It was different from the other planets in the solar system. It was the smallest. Its moon, Charon, did not orbit Pluto, but instead the two together orbited the same spot in space. Pluto also had a much more **elliptical** orbit than the other planets of the solar system. This means that at times it travels closer to the sun than Neptune, moving more like a comet than a planet.

The Kuiper Belt

Gerard Kuiper thought there might be a second area of the solar system that was filled with small objects, like the asteroid belt. Scientists thought this was likely because our solar system began as a giant dust cloud. The pieces of dust then clumped together to become our sun and the planets of our solar system. The asteroid belt formed when Mars and Jupiter took up most of the dust, preventing a new planet forming. Scientists realized that the Kuiper belt could be a second area of leftover, clumped-up pieces of dust.

The Kuiper belt was too far away for telescopes in 1950 to see. By the 1990s, with powerful telescopes, scientists began to find Kuiper belt objects. Some of them were almost as big as Pluto. When astronomers discovered Eris, a Kuiper belt object larger than Pluto, 6.2 billion miles (10 billion km) from the sun, they had to decide whether Eris was our solar system's tenth planet. But, there were many more similar objects in the area. Were all these objects planets?

Voting Over Pluto

In 2006, the International Astronomers Union (IAU) voted to change the definition of a planet. They said that a planet must have cleared its neighborhood of other objects. Pluto had not done that, so it was put into a new category, "**dwarf planets**." The scientists said that although Pluto and other dwarf planets like Eris were different from other asteroids, they were also different from the other planets in the solar system. Therefore, Pluto could not be a planet.

SPACE DISCOVERY

BY 2016, SCIENTISTS OFFICIALLY RECOGNIZED FIVE DWARF PLANETS IN OUR SOLAR SYSTEM: PLUTO, HAUMEA, MAKEMAKE, AND ERIS IN THE KUIPER BELT, AND CERES IN THE ASTEROID BELT. ANOTHER SIX OBJECTS IN THE KUIPER BELT ARE BEING CONSIDERED, AS THEY ARE MORE THAN 560 MILES (900 KM) IN DIAMETER. SCIENTISTS THINK THERE MAY BE AS MANY AS 100 DWARF PLANETS IN OUR SOLAR SYSTEM.

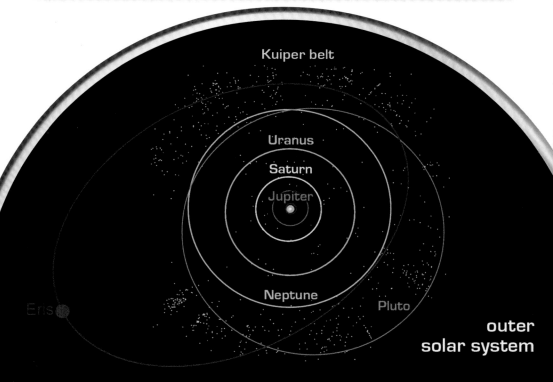

Kuiper belt

Uranus

Saturn

Jupiter

Neptune

Pluto

Eris

outer
solar system

Eris takes 560.9 years to orbit our sun. Its elliptical orbit, seen here, sometimes brings it as close to the sun as Neptune.

Building New Horizons

To build *New Horizons*, NASA scientists and engineers had to design a robot that could survive decades in space. It also had to be large enough to carry what it needed to get to Pluto, and the instruments it needed to explore when it got there. Another factor was that it had to be light enough to be launched from Earth.

Size and Power

Scientists designed a spacecraft about the size of a large piano, weighing 1,054 pounds (478 kg). Because it would travel far from the sun, it could not rely on solar panels to provide power, so instead it used a small nuclear battery that could power the robot for almost 20 years.

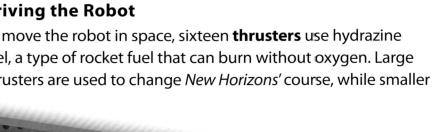

Driving the Robot

To move the robot in space, sixteen **thrusters** use hydrazine fuel, a type of rocket fuel that can burn without oxygen. Large thrusters are used to change *New Horizons'* course, while smaller ones spin it in place. This allows it to look at things and aim its **antennae** back at Earth. Two sun **sensors** focus on the sun, to tell the robot where it is and which end is "up." This allows the robot to aim its equipment at the right spot. *New Horizons* has four computers. One controls the robot's flight through space. The other controls its scientific equipment and sends messages back to Earth through the antennae. The two other computers are exact copies of the first two. If something goes wrong with the first two computers, NASA has backups.

New Horizons is designed to look at many different things before turning its antennae (top) to send signals back to Earth.

SPACE DISCOVERY

NEW HORIZONS IS A ROBOT BECAUSE IT HAS A COMPUTER THAT CAN LOOK AT DATA AND DECIDE WHAT TO DO. PLUTO IS SO FAR FROM EARTH THAT RADIO SIGNALS TAKE 4.5 HOURS TO GET THERE. IF NEW HORIZONS HAS A PROBLEM, IT WOULD TAKE AT LEAST 9 HOURS FOR EARTH TO COME UP WITH A SOLUTION. AS A RESULT, THE COMPUTER HAS TO MAKE A LOT OF DECISIONS ON ITS OWN.

Scientific Equipment

New Horizons has seven measuring and recording devices in total. One of these is the Long Range Reconnaissance Imager (LORRI), which is a camera that can take photographs in visible light. To make sure the camera's images are in focus, the camera is kept chilled and insulated, or separate. This makes sure that any differences in temperature along the length of the camera do not cause parts of it to expand, which would make pictures out of focus.

Two other devices also record information on board New Horizons. They are nicknamed Ralph and Alice, after two characters in an old television show called The Honeymooners. Ralph takes pictures in visible light and sees things in **infrared**. Alice is an **ultraviolet** imaging **spectrometer**, which looks at how ultraviolet light changes as it moves through Pluto's **atmosphere**. This gives scientists clues about what Pluto's atmosphere is made of.

Ralph weighs 22.7 pounds (10.3 kg). Its magnifying telescope can see 10 times better than the human eye.

Ralph mapped Pluto. The purple areas are rich in methane ice.

Measuring Space

New Horizons also has the Solar Wind at Pluto (SWAP) and the Pluto Energetic Particle Spectrometer Science Investigation (PEPSSI) devices. These look at the energy in space around Pluto, measuring particles, or tiny pieces of matter, produced by the sun that create the **solar wind**, and **high-energy particles** from outer space. We can see the solar wind when it hits the Earth in the form of the northern and southern lights at Earth's poles. Scientists wanted to discover what the solar wind was like so far away at Pluto.

Two other devices include the Venetia Burney Student Dust Collector to measure dust around Pluto, and the Radioscience Experiment (REX), which scans Pluto to measure the planet's temperature and atmosphere.

SPACE FIRST

NEW HORIZONS ALSO CONTAINS THE ASHES OF CLYDE TOMBAUGH, THE MAN WHO DISCOVERED PLUTO. HE DIED IN 1997, NINE YEARS BEFORE *NEW HORIZONS* LAUNCHED. THE CANISTER BEARS THE INSCRIPTION "INTERNED HEREIN ARE REMAINS OF AMERICAN CLYDE W. TOMBAUGH, DISCOVERER OF PLUTO AND THE SOLAR SYSTEM'S 'THIRD ZONE.' ADELLE AND MURON'S BOY, PATRICIA'S HUSBAND, ANNETTE AND ALDEN'S FATHER, ASTRONOMER, TEACHER, PUNSTER, AND FRIEND: CLYDE W. TOMBAUGH (1906–1997)."

Countdown to Launch

Once *New Horizons* was built, it was flown to the Kennedy Space Center, in Florida, on September 24, 2005. The robot was loaded onto an Atlas V rocket for a launch date of January 11, 2006. However, problems with the rocket delayed the launch by a week.

Takeoff

NASA scientists worried about the launch delay. Although there were backup times for launches in February, the robot had to launch before January 23 to be able to reach Jupiter. There, it would use the gravity of the planet to speed up. This would then shorten the robot's trip to Pluto. Fortunately, there were no additional delays and on January 19, 2006, *New Horizons* was launched from Cape Canaveral.

Signals to Earth

Launching *New Horizons* was only the first step, however. NASA waited anxiously until the robot's computer woke up and sent a signal to Earth. Once they received that signal, they knew the robot was working, and on its way to Pluto. On January 28, 2006, and again on January 30, NASA controllers guided *New Horizons* through course corrections. Starting February 20, 2006, NASA began a week-long test of *New Horizons'* scientific instruments. On April 7, 2006, *New Horizons* passed the orbit of Mars.

SPACE FIRST

NEW HORIZONS WAS THE FASTEST SPACECRAFT EVER LAUNCHED USING FIVE-STAGE ROCKET BOOSTERS. THESE LAUNCHED THE ROBOT AT 36,373 MILES (58,530 KM) PER HOUR. IT PASSED THE ORBIT OF THE MOON IN 9 HOURS, A JOURNEY THAT TOOK THE *APOLLO* MISSION, IN 1969, 3 DAYS! IT THEN PASSED CLOSE TO THE SUN, USING THE SUN'S GRAVITY TO SPEED UP EVEN MORE. BY THE TIME *NEW HORIZONS* PASSED MARS, IT WAS TRAVELING AT MORE THAN 47,000 (75,640 KM) MILES PER HOUR.

This Atlas V rocket launched *New Horizons* into space.

Encounter with Jupiter

On September 4, 2006, *New Horizons* took its first picture of Jupiter. It was 181 million miles (291 million km) away from the planet, but approaching fast. *New Horizons* was visiting Jupiter to use the pull of the planet's gravity to speed up. This would shorten the trip to Pluto by three years. It was also an excellent chance to research the solar system's largest planet.

The Jupiter flyby was a great chance to test *New Horizons'* equipment.

By January 2007, *New Horizons* was close enough to Jupiter to start taking pictures of its moons. The moons were not in a good position for closeup shots, but *New Horizons'* instruments were designed to take pictures of distant and dim objects. They took pictures of Ganymede, Europa, and Calisto. They even spotted a volcanic eruption on Io, sending a plume more than 205 miles (330 km) high. *New Horizons* also took one of the closest shots of Jupiter's Little Red Spot. This is a storm similar to Jupiter's Great Red Spot, but smaller, at only 70 percent the size of Earth.

To the Largest Planet

On February 28, 2007, *New Horizons* came within 1.4 million miles (2.25 million km) of Jupiter, making its closest approach to the planet. Like a skateboarder pulling against a faster skateboarder to pick up speed, *New Horizons* sped up by another 9,000 miles (14,480 km) per hour. It reached a speed of 51,000 miles (82,080 km) per hour. This move, called a gravity assist, shortened the voyage to Pluto by three years.

After leaving Jupiter, *New Horizons* went into hibernation, allowing it to save energy for the trip to Pluto. Even though it was asleep, the robot was programmed to wake for two months each year to check its equipment and send messages back to Earth.

Waking Up to Pluto

New Horizons passed the orbit of Saturn on June 8, 2008, and Uranus on March 18, 2011. The robot continued to travel onward, mostly asleep, occasionally waking up to tell NASA that it was okay. In 2012, NASA activated the SWAP and PEPSS devices as well as the dust collector. They did so to test the equipment and gather information about the **heliosphere**, measuring the effects of the sun at that part of the solar system. The tests also allowed NASA to see how much fuel New Horizons still had, and how long the robot could continue its mission.

Wakey, Wakey!

On January 4, 2015, New Horizons woke again from hibernation. One month later, NASA released pictures of Pluto as New Horizons got closer. The robot was still more than 125 million miles (77 million km) away from the planet, but more details about Pluto were coming clear. By April 15, pictures of Pluto suggested the planet had a polar ice cap.

Close to Arrival

NASA scientists were working hard, preparing the systems and calculating the best route past Pluto for New Horizons to take. Everyone was excited that, after almost a decade, the robot would finally arrive at the dwarf planet.

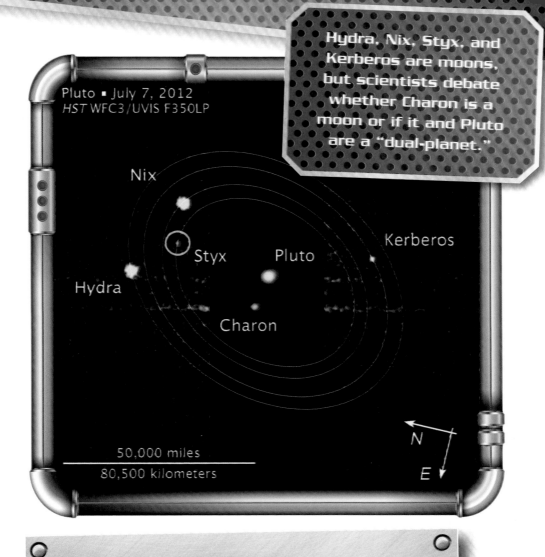

Pluto • July 7, 2012
HST WFC3/UVIS F350LP

Nix

Styx

Pluto

Kerberos

Hydra

Charon

50,000 miles
80,500 kilometers

N

E

Hydra, Nix, Styx, and Kerberos are moons, but scientists debate whether Charon is a moon or if it and Pluto are a "dual-planet."

SPACE DISCOVERY

WHEN *NEW HORIZONS* WAS LAUNCHED, SCIENTISTS HAD SEEN VERY LITTLE OF PLUTO, EVEN THROUGH TELESCOPES. WHILE *NEW HORIZONS* WAS IN HIBERNATION, THEY DISCOVERED TWO NEW MOONS ORBITING PLUTO, KERBEROS AND STYX. NASA THEN USED COMPUTER CALCULATIONS TO FIGURE OUT WHETHER *NEW HORIZONS* MIGHT CRASH INTO AN UNEXPECTED OBJECT NEAR PLUTO. EVEN A SMALL SPECK OF DUST TRAVELING 15.5 MILES (25 KM) PER SECOND COULD HIT *NEW HORIZONS* WITH THE FORCE OF A BULLET!

Software Glitch!

In June and July, *New Horizons* snapped more pictures of Pluto. Then, on July 4, 2015, *New Horizons* suddenly stopped sending data back to Earth. NASA scientists frantically tried to find out what was wrong. They contacted *New Horizons'* backup computer and figured out that the main computer had run into a software glitch. It had gone into "safe mode" and shut down all nonessential systems.

Fortunately, NASA had a backup computer just in case things like this happened. Using the backup computer, scientists discovered a problem in the programming that had caused two tasks to take place at once. This had overloaded the robot. They were then able to upload a fix to *New Horizons*. Normal operations resumed on July 7, one week before *New Horizons'* closest approach to Pluto.

Mission Objectives

New Horizons had traveled closer to Pluto than any other robot before it. Therefore, there was a lot about the planet that NASA scientists wanted the robot to find out. However, *New Horizons* was traveling so fast, it was impossible for it to slow down enough to orbit Pluto. NASA had to figure out exactly what they wanted out of the mission. Most important was to take pictures of and map Pluto and Charon.

The robot also had to get data about the makeup of Pluto and Charon's surfaces and of Pluto's atmosphere. They also wanted to see if Charon had any atmosphere, map surface temperatures, and map the surfaces of the four other moons of Pluto.

SPACE DISCOVERY

DESPITE ITS SMALL SIZE, PLUTO HAS AN ATMOSPHERE, MADE MOSTLY OF NITROGEN, CARBON MONOXIDE, AND METHANE. THIS VARIES A LOT OVER PLUTO'S 246-YEAR-LONG ORBIT. DURING ITS "WINTER," IT IS 50 TIMES FARTHER FROM THE SUN THAN EARTH, AND THE ATMOSPHERE FREEZES. IN THE SUMMER, PLUTO MOVES TO JUST 30 TIMES THE DISTANCE OF EARTH FROM THE SUN. THIS IS CLOSE ENOUGH TO RAISE PLUTO'S SURFACE TEMPERATURE FOR THE ATMOSPHERE TO THAW.

New Horizons took this photo of Pluto 15 minutes after its closest approach.

Pluto Encounter

As *New Horizons* made its closest approach to Pluto on July 14, 2015, the robot entered a 22-hour-long period of radio silence, when no communication was made. The robot had to pay attention to Pluto, now just 7,750 miles (12,470 km) away, and that meant its antenna could no longer point toward Earth. All the time, the robot was doing what it was programmed to do, snapping pictures, taking measurements, and collecting data. NASA scientists could only wait. Scientists had figured out that there was only a 1-in-10,000 chance that *New Horizons* could hit a piece of space debris during the flyby. Although this was unlikely, NASA still nervously waited for *New Horizons* to radio back to Earth.

Mission Accomplished

Finally, on July 15, a signal from *New Horizons* reached Earth. The robot was healthy, and the data was collected. NASA scientists celebrated.

New Horizons traveled past Pluto at a relative speed of 8.56 miles (13.78 km) per second. It came within 17,900 miles (28,810 km) of Pluto's moon Charon. It was able to map both Pluto and Charon in detail. LORRI was able to snap more detailed pictures. Alice measured the atmosphere, while SWAP and PEPSSI sampled it and measured how it was affected by the solar wind. *New Horizons* was also able to accurately measure Pluto's diameter and **mass**.

SPACE DISCOVERY

NEW HORIZONS COLLECTED MORE THAN 50 GIGABITS OF DATA DURING ITS PLUTO FLYBY. HOWEVER, IT WILL TAKE MORE THAN 18 MONTHS FOR NEW HORIZONS TO SEND ALL OF ITS DATA BACK TO EARTH. NOT ONLY DOES THE DISTANCE TO THE ROBOT MEAN THAT IT TAKES 4.5 HOURS FOR SIGNALS TO REACH EARTH, VERY LITTLE OF THOSE SIGNALS GET THROUGH.

New Horizons captured this extremely clear image of Pluto's largest moon, Charon.

Amazing Pluto

Pluto may be a dwarf planet, but it has provided scientists with countless amazing discoveries. One of the biggest surprises is that Pluto has water and blue skies. *New Horizons* took a photo of Pluto's atmosphere that showed a blue haze. This is likely to be a result of the sun's ultraviolet radiation smashing into Pluto's atmosphere. This creates complicated **molecules** that scatter the sun's light, in much the same way that Earth's atmosphere scatters sunlight, creating our blue sky.

Pluto's light, heart-shaped area was named Tombaugh Regio in honor of Clyde Tombaugh.

The surface of Pluto is full of variations. They include a bright, heart-shaped feature surrounded by mountains more than 11,000 feet (3,353 m) high. Scientists estimate these mountains are only 100 million years old, which is quite young considering the solar system is more than 4.5 billion years old. Scientists wonder what caused these mountains to form, and some think the mountains might even be ice volcanoes!

Amazing Moons

New Horizons also gave scientists a close look at Pluto's moon Charon. They could see that the moon has a young and varied surface like Pluto, including mountain ranges more than 600 miles (966 km) long and a long canyon 4–6 miles (6–10 km) deep. Charon also has an atmosphere, and an area of ammonia near one of the moon's larger craters. Scientists do not know what could be producing the ammonia, but are excited to find out. Water ice was found on Charon, and on Pluto's other moons.

As of 2016, scientists are still downloading *New Horizons'* data, and they still have to work through all of it. *New Horizons'* discoveries will continue to come in for years to come.

SPACE DISCOVERY

DESPITE ITS SPEED, NEW HORIZONS WILL NEVER CATCH VOYAGER 1 OR 2 BECAUSE THEY ARE JOURNEYING THROUGH SPACE EVEN MORE QUICKLY THAN NEW HORIZONS, AND ARE MANY MILES AHEAD OF THE ROBOT.

The Mission Continues

As of January 2016, *New Horizons* was more than 128 million miles (206 million km) from Pluto, and heading deeper into the Kuiper belt. As *New Horizons* approached Pluto, scientists looked to see where the robot could visit next. The location depended partly on how much fuel the robot had left. In the meantime, *New Horizons* continued to collect data. On December 2, 2015, LORRI snapped a picture of Kuiper Belt Object 1994 JR1 from 170 million miles (273.6 million km) away. This was close enough to show the shape of the object and some details of its surface.

Looking Ahead

New Horizons will pass near Kuiper Belt Object 2014 MU69 in January 2019. Its instruments will continue to work until its battery dies out in 2026. NASA's next missions on the New Frontiers program include a visit to Jupiter and to Venus.

New Horizons has created a lot of excitement around Pluto and the Kuiper belt, and scientists are eager to learn more about this mysterious region of the solar system. It takes a lot of patience and planning to make a mission like *New Horizons* come about. However, thanks to the scientists who designed it, planned its launch, and guided its journey through space, that patience has paid off. We have learned more about the farthest reaches of the solar system than Clyde Tombaugh could have thought possible.

SPACE FIRST

ON AUGUST 28, 2015, NASA SCIENTISTS SETTLED ON A 30-MILE (48 KM) WIDE KUIPER BELT OBJECT KNOWN AS 2014 MU69 AS *NEW HORIZONS'* NEXT DESTINATION. IT WAS DIRECTED TOWARD THE OBJECT IN LATE OCTOBER. *NEW HORIZONS* IS EXPECTED TO FLY BY THE OBJECT ON JANUARY 1, 2019, AND MAY PASS EVEN CLOSER TO IT THAN IT DID TO PLUTO.

Kuiper Be
Object 201
MU69 was fi
discovered
2014, by th
Hubble Spac
Telescope,

GLOSSARY

antennae Devices that send and receive radio signals.

asteroid belt An area between the orbits of Mars and Jupiter where lots of asteroids are found.

atmosphere A layer of gases that surround a planet or moon.

data Information.

dwarf planets Objects that orbit the sun, have an almost round shape, have not cleared the neighborhood around their orbits, and are not moons.

elliptical Shaped like an egg.

flyby When a spacecraft flies close to a planet or moon in order to gain extra momentum from it.

heliosphere The area of space in our solar system influenced by the sun's solar wind.

hibernation A state in which all nonessential systems in a spacecraft are switched off temporarily to save energy.

high-energy particles Small pieces of matter carrying a lot of energy, like an X-ray.

infrared A form of light invisible to the human eye.

Kuiper belt An area of our solar system beyond Neptune's orbit made of small rocky and icy objects.

mass The amount of matter that makes up an object.

molecules The smallest amounts of chemical compounds that can exist.

orbit To travel around an object in a circular way.

robots Machines that are programmed to carry out particular jobs.

sensors Devices that react to particular aspects of the environment, such as light waves.

solar wind The flow of charged particles from the sun.

spectrometer A machine that identifies the makeup of an object by seeing how it interacts with light.

thrusters Small engines that are used to change the direction or speed of a spacecraft.

ultraviolet An invisible form of energy.

FOR MORE INFORMATION

Books

Glaser, Chayer. *Pluto: The Icy Dwarf Planet* (Out of This World). New York, NY: Bearport Publishing, 2015.

Kahn, Katie. *A Space Explorer's Guide to Pluto (Volume 9)*. Seattle, WA: CreateSpace, 2015.

Kops, Deborah. *Exploring Space Robots*. Minneapolis, MN: Lerner Publishing, 2011.

Kortenkamp, Steve. *Demoting Pluto: The Discovery of the Dwarf Planets*. Mankato, MN: Capstone, 2015.

Websites

Due to the changing nature of Internet links, PowerKids Press has developed an online list of websites related to the subject of this book. This site is updated regularly. Please use this link to access the list: **www.powerkidslinks.com/res/newh**

INDEX